50 Delicious Shake Recipes for Home

By: Kelly Johnson

Table of Contents

- Berry Bliss Shake
- Mango Coconut Delight
- Chocolate Almond Dream
- Matcha Mint Shake
- Tropical Pineapple Paradise
- Peanut Butter Banana Bliss
- Green Goddess Smoothie
- Strawberry Cheesecake Shake
- Espresso Mocha Magic
- Vanilla Chai Infusion
- Caramel Apple Crunch
- Blueberry Almond Fusion
- Hazelnut Mocha Marvel
- Cinnamon Roll Shake
- Tiramisu Temptation
- Pumpkin Spice Indulgence
- Raspberry Lemonade Zing
- Chocolate Cherry Jubilee
- Pina Colada Protein Punch
- Kale Pineapple Green Shake
- Almond Joy Smoothie
- Peach Cobbler Shake
- Matcha Mango Meltdown
- Coconut Vanilla Bean Dream
- Salted Caramel Pretzel Shake
- Avocado Banana Cream
- Mocha Hazelnut Fantasy
- Berry Coconut Breeze
- Chocolate Peanut Butter Crunch
- Apple Cinnamon Delight
- Cherry Almond Bliss
- Lemon Basil Mint Smoothie

- Maple Pecan Protein Shake
- Sweet Potato Pie Shake
- Pomegranate Acai Burst
- Strawberry Rhubarb Shake
- Mint Chocolate Chip Shake
- Spiced Orange Creamsicle
- Tropical Guava Dream
- Vanilla Nutmeg Bliss
- Raspberry Coconut Fusion
- White Chocolate Raspberry
- Blackberry Lemon Basil
- Chocolate Banana Nut
- Fig and Walnut Shake
- Gingerbread Protein Shake
- Coconut Matcha Bliss
- Spicy Mango Tango
- Blueberry Yogurt Smoothie
- Nutty Almond Joy Shake

Berry Bliss Shake

Ingredients:

- 1 cup mixed berries (such as strawberries, blueberries, raspberries, and blackberries)
- 1/2 cup Greek yogurt (vanilla or plain)
- 1/2 cup almond milk (or your preferred milk)
- 1 tablespoon honey or maple syrup (adjust to taste)
- 1/2 teaspoon vanilla extract
- 1/4 cup rolled oats (optional, for added texture and fiber)
- Ice cubes (as needed)

Instructions:

1. **Blend Ingredients:** In a blender, combine the mixed berries, Greek yogurt, almond milk, honey or maple syrup, and vanilla extract. If using rolled oats, add them as well.
2. **Add Ice:** Add a few ice cubes to the blender for a chilled, thick texture.
3. **Blend:** Blend on high until smooth and creamy. If the shake is too thick, add more almond milk or a bit of water to reach your desired consistency.
4. **Taste and Adjust:** Taste the shake and adjust sweetness if needed by adding a little more honey or maple syrup.
5. **Serve:** Pour the shake into a glass and enjoy immediately. Optionally, garnish with extra berries on top.

Enjoy your Berry Bliss Shake! It's a refreshing and nutritious treat perfect for any time of the day.

Mango Coconut Delight

Ingredients:

- 1 cup fresh or frozen mango chunks
- 1/2 cup coconut milk (full-fat or light, depending on preference)
- 1/4 cup Greek yogurt (plain or vanilla)
- 1 tablespoon honey or agave syrup (adjust to taste)
- 1/4 cup shredded coconut (toasted or plain)
- 1/2 teaspoon vanilla extract
- Ice cubes (as needed)

Instructions:

1. **Blend Ingredients:** In a blender, combine the mango chunks, coconut milk, Greek yogurt, honey or agave syrup, shredded coconut, and vanilla extract.
2. **Add Ice:** If using fresh mango, add a handful of ice cubes to the blender for a thicker, chilled shake.
3. **Blend:** Blend on high until smooth and creamy. If the shake is too thick, add more coconut milk or a bit of water to reach your desired consistency.
4. **Taste and Adjust:** Taste the shake and adjust sweetness if needed by adding more honey or agave syrup.
5. **Serve:** Pour the shake into a glass and garnish with a sprinkle of shredded coconut on top if desired. Serve immediately.

Enjoy your Mango Coconut Delight! It's a tropical treat that's both creamy and refreshing.

Chocolate Almond Dream

Ingredients:

- 1 cup almond milk (or your preferred milk)
- 1/2 cup Greek yogurt (plain or vanilla)
- 1/4 cup almond butter (or almond paste)
- 2 tablespoons cocoa powder (unsweetened)
- 2 tablespoons honey or maple syrup (adjust to taste)
- 1/4 cup almonds (toasted or raw, plus extra for garnish)
- 1/4 teaspoon vanilla extract
- Ice cubes (as needed)

Instructions:

1. **Blend Ingredients:** In a blender, combine the almond milk, Greek yogurt, almond butter, cocoa powder, honey or maple syrup, almonds, and vanilla extract.
2. **Add Ice:** Add a few ice cubes to the blender if you prefer a thicker, colder shake.
3. **Blend:** Blend on high until smooth and creamy. If the shake is too thick, add more almond milk or a bit of water to adjust the consistency.
4. **Taste and Adjust:** Taste the shake and adjust sweetness if needed by adding more honey or maple syrup.
5. **Serve:** Pour the shake into a glass and garnish with extra almonds if desired. Serve immediately.

Enjoy your Chocolate Almond Dream shake! It's a decadent treat with a delicious blend of chocolate and almond flavors.

Matcha Mint Shake

Ingredients:

- 1 cup almond milk (or your preferred milk)
- 1/2 cup Greek yogurt (plain or vanilla)
- 1 tablespoon matcha green tea powder
- 1/4 cup fresh mint leaves (packed)
- 1-2 tablespoons honey or maple syrup (adjust to taste)
- 1/4 teaspoon vanilla extract
- Ice cubes (as needed)

Instructions:

1. **Prepare Ingredients:** If using fresh mint leaves, gently muddle them to release their flavor. You can do this in the blender or with a muddler before blending.
2. **Blend Ingredients:** In a blender, combine the almond milk, Greek yogurt, matcha powder, mint leaves, honey or maple syrup, and vanilla extract.
3. **Add Ice:** Add a handful of ice cubes for a cooler, thicker shake.
4. **Blend:** Blend on high until smooth and creamy. If the shake is too thick, add more almond milk or a bit of water to reach your desired consistency.
5. **Taste and Adjust:** Taste the shake and adjust sweetness if needed by adding more honey or maple syrup.
6. **Serve:** Pour the shake into a glass and garnish with a few extra mint leaves if desired. Serve immediately.

Enjoy your Matcha Mint Shake! It's a vibrant and refreshing shake with the perfect blend of matcha and mint flavors.

Tropical Pineapple Paradise

Ingredients:

- 1 cup fresh or frozen pineapple chunks
- 1/2 cup coconut milk (full-fat or light, depending on preference)
- 1/2 cup Greek yogurt (plain or vanilla)
- 1/4 cup orange juice
- 1 tablespoon honey or agave syrup (adjust to taste)
- 1/2 teaspoon vanilla extract
- 1/4 cup shredded coconut (optional, for added texture)
- Ice cubes (as needed)

Instructions:

1. **Blend Ingredients:** In a blender, combine the pineapple chunks, coconut milk, Greek yogurt, orange juice, honey or agave syrup, and vanilla extract.
2. **Add Ice:** If using fresh pineapple, add a handful of ice cubes to the blender for a thicker, chilled shake.
3. **Blend:** Blend on high until smooth and creamy. If the shake is too thick, add more coconut milk or a bit of water to reach your desired consistency.
4. **Taste and Adjust:** Taste the shake and adjust sweetness if needed by adding more honey or agave syrup.
5. **Serve:** Pour the shake into a glass and optionally garnish with shredded coconut. Serve immediately.

Enjoy your Tropical Pineapple Paradise! It's a delicious, tropical escape in a glass that's both creamy and refreshing.

Peanut Butter Banana Bliss

Ingredients:

- 1 large ripe banana (peeled)
- 2 tablespoons peanut butter (creamy or chunky, depending on preference)
- 1 cup milk (almond, soy, or dairy)
- 1/2 cup Greek yogurt (plain or vanilla)
- 1 tablespoon honey or maple syrup (adjust to taste)
- 1/4 teaspoon vanilla extract
- Ice cubes (as needed)

Instructions:

1. **Blend Ingredients:** In a blender, combine the banana, peanut butter, milk, Greek yogurt, honey or maple syrup, and vanilla extract.
2. **Add Ice:** Add a handful of ice cubes for a thicker, colder shake.
3. **Blend:** Blend on high until smooth and creamy. If the shake is too thick, add more milk to achieve your desired consistency.
4. **Taste and Adjust:** Taste the shake and adjust sweetness if needed by adding more honey or maple syrup.
5. **Serve:** Pour the shake into a glass and enjoy immediately.

Enjoy your Peanut Butter Banana Bliss shake! It's a delicious, creamy blend of banana and peanut butter that's perfect for a quick breakfast or a satisfying snack.

Green Goddess Smoothie

Ingredients:

- 1 cup spinach (fresh or frozen)
- 1/2 cup kale (stems removed, fresh or frozen)
- 1/2 ripe avocado
- 1 small green apple (cored and chopped)
- 1/2 cucumber (peeled and chopped)
- 1 tablespoon chia seeds or flaxseeds
- 1 cup coconut water (or your preferred liquid)
- 1 tablespoon honey or agave syrup (adjust to taste)
- 1/2 teaspoon lemon juice
- Ice cubes (as needed)

Instructions:

1. **Prepare Ingredients:** If using fresh spinach and kale, rinse them thoroughly. Peel and chop the cucumber and apple.

2. **Blend Ingredients:** In a blender, combine the spinach, kale, avocado, green apple, cucumber, chia seeds or flaxseeds, coconut water, honey or agave syrup, and lemon juice.
3. **Add Ice:** Add a handful of ice cubes for a cooler, thicker smoothie.
4. **Blend:** Blend on high until smooth and creamy. If the smoothie is too thick, add more coconut water or a bit of water to reach your desired consistency.
5. **Taste and Adjust:** Taste the smoothie and adjust sweetness or lemon juice if needed.
6. **Serve:** Pour the smoothie into a glass and enjoy immediately.

Enjoy your Green Goddess Smoothie! It's a nutrient-packed, refreshing drink that's perfect for a boost of energy and vitality.

Strawberry Cheesecake Shake

Ingredients:

- 1 cup fresh or frozen strawberries (hulled)
- 1/2 cup Greek yogurt (plain or vanilla)
- 1/4 cup cream cheese (softened)
- 1/2 cup milk (dairy or non-dairy)
- 2 tablespoons honey or maple syrup (adjust to taste)
- 1/2 teaspoon vanilla extract
- 1/4 cup graham cracker crumbs (optional, for a cheesecake touch)
- Ice cubes (as needed)

Instructions:

1. **Prepare Ingredients:** If using fresh strawberries, rinse and hull them. Soften the cream cheese by letting it sit at room temperature or briefly microwaving it.
2. **Blend Ingredients:** In a blender, combine the strawberries, Greek yogurt, cream cheese, milk, honey or maple syrup, and vanilla extract.
3. **Add Ice:** Add a handful of ice cubes for a thicker, chilled shake. If you're using graham cracker crumbs, add a couple of tablespoons to the blender for a more authentic cheesecake flavor.
4. **Blend:** Blend on high until smooth and creamy. If the shake is too thick, add more milk to achieve your desired consistency.
5. **Taste and Adjust:** Taste the shake and adjust sweetness if needed by adding more honey or maple syrup.
6. **Serve:** Pour the shake into a glass. Optionally, garnish with extra graham cracker crumbs on top for added texture and a cheesecake feel.

Enjoy your Strawberry Cheesecake Shake! It's a creamy and indulgent treat that brings the classic cheesecake flavor into a refreshing shake.

Espresso Mocha Magic

Ingredients:

- 1 cup brewed espresso or strong coffee (cooled)
- 1/2 cup milk (dairy or non-dairy, such as almond or oat milk)
- 2 tablespoons cocoa powder (unsweetened)
- 2 tablespoons honey or maple syrup (adjust to taste)
- 1/4 cup Greek yogurt (plain or vanilla)
- 1/4 teaspoon vanilla extract
- Ice cubes (as needed)
- Whipped cream (optional, for topping)
- Chocolate shavings or cocoa powder (optional, for garnish)

Instructions:

1. **Prepare Espresso:** Brew a cup of espresso or strong coffee and let it cool to room temperature.
2. **Blend Ingredients:** In a blender, combine the cooled espresso, milk, cocoa powder, honey or maple syrup, Greek yogurt, and vanilla extract.
3. **Add Ice:** Add a handful of ice cubes for a thicker, colder shake.
4. **Blend:** Blend on high until smooth and creamy. If the shake is too thick, add a bit more milk to reach your desired consistency.
5. **Taste and Adjust:** Taste the shake and adjust sweetness or cocoa powder if needed.
6. **Serve:** Pour the shake into a glass. Optionally, top with whipped cream and garnish with chocolate shavings or a sprinkle of cocoa powder.

Enjoy your Espresso Mocha Magic! It's a delicious blend of rich espresso and chocolate that's perfect for a pick-me-up or an indulgent treat.

Vanilla Chai Infusion

Ingredients:

- 1 cup milk (dairy or non-dairy, such as almond or oat milk)
- 1/2 cup Greek yogurt (plain or vanilla)
- 1 tablespoon chai tea concentrate (or 1-2 chai tea bags brewed and cooled)
- 1 tablespoon honey or maple syrup (adjust to taste)
- 1/2 teaspoon vanilla extract
- 1/4 teaspoon ground cinnamon
- 1/4 teaspoon ground cardamom (optional, for extra chai flavor)
- Ice cubes (as needed)
- Cinnamon stick or ground cinnamon (for garnish, optional)

Instructions:

1. **Prepare Chai Tea:** If using chai tea bags, brew a strong cup of chai tea and let it cool. If using chai tea concentrate, measure out 1 tablespoon.
2. **Blend Ingredients:** In a blender, combine the milk, Greek yogurt, cooled chai tea or chai concentrate, honey or maple syrup, vanilla extract, ground cinnamon, and ground cardamom (if using).
3. **Add Ice:** Add a handful of ice cubes for a thicker, chilled shake.
4. **Blend:** Blend on high until smooth and creamy. If the shake is too thick, add more milk to reach your desired consistency.
5. **Taste and Adjust:** Taste the shake and adjust sweetness or spice if needed.
6. **Serve:** Pour the shake into a glass. Optionally, garnish with a cinnamon stick or a sprinkle of ground cinnamon on top.

Enjoy your Vanilla Chai Infusion! It's a creamy, spiced shake that combines the comforting flavors of chai tea with the smoothness of vanilla.

Caramel Apple Crunch

Ingredients:

- 1 large apple (cored and chopped; use a sweet variety like Honeycrisp or Fuji)
- 1/2 cup Greek yogurt (plain or vanilla)
- 1/2 cup milk (dairy or non-dairy, such as almond or oat milk)
- 2 tablespoons caramel sauce (store-bought or homemade)
- 1/4 cup granola (for crunch)
- 1/4 teaspoon ground cinnamon
- 1/4 teaspoon vanilla extract
- Ice cubes (as needed)
- Extra caramel sauce (for drizzling, optional)

Instructions:

1. **Prepare Apple:** If you want a smoother texture, you can peel the apple. Core and chop it into small pieces.
2. **Blend Ingredients:** In a blender, combine the chopped apple, Greek yogurt, milk, caramel sauce, granola, ground cinnamon, and vanilla extract.
3. **Add Ice:** Add a handful of ice cubes for a colder, thicker shake.
4. **Blend:** Blend on high until smooth and creamy. If the shake is too thick, add more milk to reach your desired consistency.
5. **Taste and Adjust:** Taste the shake and adjust sweetness if needed by adding more caramel sauce.
6. **Serve:** Pour the shake into a glass. Optionally, drizzle extra caramel sauce on top and garnish with a sprinkle of granola for added crunch.

Enjoy your Caramel Apple Crunch shake! It's a creamy, indulgent treat with the sweet and comforting flavors of caramel and apple.

Blueberry Almond Fusion

Ingredients:

- 1 cup fresh or frozen blueberries
- 1/2 cup Greek yogurt (plain or vanilla)
- 1/4 cup almond butter (or almond paste)
- 1 cup almond milk (or your preferred milk)
- 1 tablespoon honey or maple syrup (adjust to taste)
- 1/4 teaspoon vanilla extract
- 1/4 cup almonds (toasted or raw, plus extra for garnish)
- Ice cubes (as needed)

Instructions:

1. **Blend Ingredients:** In a blender, combine the blueberries, Greek yogurt, almond butter, almond milk, honey or maple syrup, and vanilla extract.
2. **Add Ice:** Add a handful of ice cubes for a thicker, chilled shake.
3. **Blend:** Blend on high until smooth and creamy. If the shake is too thick, add more almond milk to reach your desired consistency.
4. **Taste and Adjust:** Taste the shake and adjust sweetness if needed by adding more honey or maple syrup.
5. **Serve:** Pour the shake into a glass. Optionally, garnish with a few extra almonds on top for added crunch.

Enjoy your Blueberry Almond Fusion shake! It's a deliciously creamy blend with the vibrant flavor of blueberries and the rich, nutty taste of almonds.

Hazelnut Mocha Marvel

Ingredients:

- 1 cup brewed coffee or espresso (cooled)
- 1/2 cup milk (dairy or non-dairy, such as almond or oat milk)
- 2 tablespoons cocoa powder (unsweetened)
- 2 tablespoons hazelnut butter (or hazelnut spread)
- 1 tablespoon honey or maple syrup (adjust to taste)
- 1/4 teaspoon vanilla extract
- 1/4 cup Greek yogurt (plain or vanilla)
- Ice cubes (as needed)
- Whipped cream (optional, for topping)
- Crushed hazelnuts or chocolate shavings (optional, for garnish)

Instructions:

1. **Prepare Coffee:** Brew a cup of coffee or espresso and let it cool to room temperature.
2. **Blend Ingredients:** In a blender, combine the cooled coffee, milk, cocoa powder, hazelnut butter, honey or maple syrup, vanilla extract, and Greek yogurt.
3. **Add Ice:** Add a handful of ice cubes for a thicker, colder shake.
4. **Blend:** Blend on high until smooth and creamy. If the shake is too thick, add a bit more milk to achieve your desired consistency.
5. **Taste and Adjust:** Taste the shake and adjust sweetness if needed by adding more honey or maple syrup.
6. **Serve:** Pour the shake into a glass. Optionally, top with whipped cream and garnish with crushed hazelnuts or chocolate shavings.

Enjoy your Hazelnut Mocha Marvel shake! It's a decadent blend of coffee, chocolate, and hazelnuts that's perfect for a treat or a special indulgence.

Cinnamon Roll Shake

Ingredients:

- 1 cup milk (dairy or non-dairy, such as almond or oat milk)
- 1/2 cup Greek yogurt (plain or vanilla)
- 1/4 cup rolled oats
- 1 tablespoon ground cinnamon
- 1 tablespoon maple syrup or honey (adjust to taste)
- 1/2 teaspoon vanilla extract
- 1/4 teaspoon ground nutmeg (optional, for extra spice)
- Ice cubes (as needed)
- Whipped cream (optional, for topping)
- Cinnamon sugar (for garnish, optional)

Instructions:

1. **Prepare Oats:** If you prefer a smoother texture, you can soak the rolled oats in a little bit of milk for about 10 minutes before blending.
2. **Blend Ingredients:** In a blender, combine the milk, Greek yogurt, rolled oats, ground cinnamon, maple syrup or honey, vanilla extract, and ground nutmeg (if using).
3. **Add Ice:** Add a handful of ice cubes for a thicker, colder shake.
4. **Blend:** Blend on high until smooth and creamy. If the shake is too thick, add more milk to reach your desired consistency.
5. **Taste and Adjust:** Taste the shake and adjust sweetness or spice if needed.
6. **Serve:** Pour the shake into a glass. Optionally, top with whipped cream and sprinkle with cinnamon sugar for a true cinnamon roll experience.

Enjoy your Cinnamon Roll Shake! It's a comforting, creamy treat that brings the delicious flavors of a cinnamon roll into a refreshing shake.

Tiramisu Temptation

Ingredients:

- 1 cup brewed coffee or espresso (cooled)
- 1/2 cup Greek yogurt (plain or vanilla)
- 1/2 cup milk (dairy or non-dairy, such as almond or oat milk)
- 2 tablespoons mascarpone cheese (softened)
- 1 tablespoon cocoa powder (unsweetened)
- 1 tablespoon honey or maple syrup (adjust to taste)
- 1/2 teaspoon vanilla extract
- 1/4 teaspoon ground cinnamon (optional, for extra flavor)
- Ice cubes (as needed)
- Whipped cream (optional, for topping)
- Cocoa powder or chocolate shavings (for garnish, optional)

Instructions:

1. **Prepare Coffee:** Brew a cup of coffee or espresso and let it cool to room temperature.
2. **Blend Ingredients:** In a blender, combine the cooled coffee, Greek yogurt, milk, mascarpone cheese, cocoa powder, honey or maple syrup, vanilla extract, and ground cinnamon (if using).
3. **Add Ice:** Add a handful of ice cubes for a thicker, colder shake.
4. **Blend:** Blend on high until smooth and creamy. If the shake is too thick, add a bit more milk to achieve your desired consistency.
5. **Taste and Adjust:** Taste the shake and adjust sweetness or cocoa powder if needed.
6. **Serve:** Pour the shake into a glass. Optionally, top with whipped cream and garnish with a dusting of cocoa powder or chocolate shavings.

Enjoy your Tiramisu Temptation shake! It's a creamy, indulgent treat that combines the rich, coffee-soaked flavors of tiramisu with the convenience of a shake.

Pumpkin Spice Indulgence

Ingredients:

- 1/2 cup canned pumpkin puree (not pumpkin pie filling)
- 1/2 cup Greek yogurt (plain or vanilla)
- 1 cup milk (dairy or non-dairy, such as almond or oat milk)
- 1/4 cup maple syrup or honey (adjust to taste)
- 1 teaspoon pumpkin pie spice (or a blend of cinnamon, nutmeg, and ginger)
- 1/2 teaspoon vanilla extract
- Ice cubes (as needed)
- Whipped cream (optional, for topping)
- Extra pumpkin pie spice or cinnamon (for garnish, optional)

Instructions:

1. **Blend Ingredients:** In a blender, combine the pumpkin puree, Greek yogurt, milk, maple syrup or honey, pumpkin pie spice, and vanilla extract.
2. **Add Ice:** Add a handful of ice cubes for a thicker, colder shake.
3. **Blend:** Blend on high until smooth and creamy. If the shake is too thick, add more milk to achieve your desired consistency.
4. **Taste and Adjust:** Taste the shake and adjust sweetness or spice if needed.
5. **Serve:** Pour the shake into a glass. Optionally, top with whipped cream and sprinkle with extra pumpkin pie spice or cinnamon for garnish.

Enjoy your Pumpkin Spice Indulgence shake! It's a deliciously creamy treat that captures all the warm, spicy flavors of fall.

Raspberry Lemonade Zing

Ingredients:

- 1 cup fresh or frozen raspberries
- 1/2 cup Greek yogurt (plain or vanilla)
- 1/2 cup lemonade (store-bought or homemade)
- 1/4 cup milk (dairy or non-dairy, such as almond or oat milk)
- 1 tablespoon honey or agave syrup (adjust to taste)
- 1/2 teaspoon lemon zest
- 1 tablespoon fresh lemon juice
- Ice cubes (as needed)
- Fresh raspberries or lemon slices (for garnish, optional)

Instructions:

1. **Blend Ingredients:** In a blender, combine the raspberries, Greek yogurt, lemonade, milk, honey or agave syrup, lemon zest, and fresh lemon juice.
2. **Add Ice:** Add a handful of ice cubes for a thicker, colder shake.
3. **Blend:** Blend on high until smooth and creamy. If the shake is too thick, add more lemonade or milk to reach your desired consistency.
4. **Taste and Adjust:** Taste the shake and adjust sweetness or tartness if needed by adding more honey or lemon juice.
5. **Serve:** Pour the shake into a glass. Optionally, garnish with fresh raspberries or a slice of lemon.

Enjoy your Raspberry Lemonade Zing shake! It's a vibrant, tangy, and refreshing drink that combines the tartness of raspberries with the zing of lemon.

Chocolate Cherry Jubilee

Ingredients:

- 1 cup fresh or frozen cherries (pitted)
- 1/2 cup Greek yogurt (plain or vanilla)
- 1/2 cup milk (dairy or non-dairy, such as almond or oat milk)
- 2 tablespoons cocoa powder (unsweetened)
- 2 tablespoons honey or maple syrup (adjust to taste)
- 1/4 teaspoon vanilla extract
- 1/4 cup dark chocolate chips or chunks (optional, for extra chocolatey goodness)
- Ice cubes (as needed)
- Whipped cream (optional, for topping)
- Fresh cherries or chocolate shavings (for garnish, optional)

Instructions:

1. **Prepare Cherries:** If using fresh cherries, pit and chop them. If using frozen cherries, they're ready to go.
2. **Blend Ingredients:** In a blender, combine the cherries, Greek yogurt, milk, cocoa powder, honey or maple syrup, vanilla extract, and dark chocolate chips or chunks (if using).
3. **Add Ice:** Add a handful of ice cubes for a thicker, colder shake.
4. **Blend:** Blend on high until smooth and creamy. If the shake is too thick, add more milk to achieve your desired consistency.
5. **Taste and Adjust:** Taste the shake and adjust sweetness or chocolate flavor if needed by adding more honey or cocoa powder.
6. **Serve:** Pour the shake into a glass. Optionally, top with whipped cream and garnish with fresh cherries or chocolate shavings.

Enjoy your Chocolate Cherry Jubilee shake! It's a luscious treat that combines the rich flavors of chocolate with the sweet-tartness of cherries.

Pina Colada Protein Punch

Ingredients:

- 1 cup fresh or frozen pineapple chunks
- 1/2 cup coconut milk (full-fat or light, depending on preference)
- 1/2 cup Greek yogurt (plain or vanilla)
- 1 scoop vanilla protein powder (your choice of brand)
- 1 tablespoon honey or maple syrup (adjust to taste)
- 1/2 teaspoon vanilla extract
- 1/4 cup shredded coconut (optional, for extra coconut flavor)
- Ice cubes (as needed)

Instructions:

1. **Blend Ingredients:** In a blender, combine the pineapple chunks, coconut milk, Greek yogurt, vanilla protein powder, honey or maple syrup, vanilla extract, and shredded coconut (if using).
2. **Add Ice:** Add a handful of ice cubes for a thicker, colder shake.
3. **Blend:** Blend on high until smooth and creamy. If the shake is too thick, add a bit more coconut milk or water to reach your desired consistency.
4. **Taste and Adjust:** Taste the shake and adjust sweetness if needed by adding more honey or maple syrup.
5. **Serve:** Pour the shake into a glass and enjoy immediately.

Enjoy your Pina Colada Protein Punch! It's a creamy, tropical shake that combines the flavors of pineapple and coconut with a protein boost, perfect for a post-workout treat or a nutritious snack.

Kale Pineapple Green Shake

Ingredients:

- 1 cup fresh or frozen pineapple chunks
- 1 cup kale leaves (stems removed, packed)
- 1/2 banana (peeled, for added creaminess)
- 1/2 cup Greek yogurt (plain or vanilla)
- 1/2 cup coconut water (or your preferred liquid)
- 1 tablespoon honey or agave syrup (adjust to taste)
- 1/4 teaspoon vanilla extract
- Ice cubes (as needed)

Instructions:

1. **Prepare Ingredients:** If using fresh kale, wash and remove the stems. Peel and slice the banana.
2. **Blend Ingredients:** In a blender, combine the pineapple chunks, kale leaves, banana, Greek yogurt, coconut water, honey or agave syrup, and vanilla extract.
3. **Add Ice:** Add a handful of ice cubes for a thicker, colder shake.
4. **Blend:** Blend on high until smooth and creamy. If the shake is too thick, add more coconut water or a bit of water to achieve your desired consistency.
5. **Taste and Adjust:** Taste the shake and adjust sweetness if needed by adding more honey or agave syrup.
6. **Serve:** Pour the shake into a glass and enjoy immediately.

Enjoy your Kale Pineapple Green Shake! It's a vibrant and nutritious drink that combines the sweet taste of pineapple with the health benefits of kale, creating a deliciously balanced green shake.

Almond Joy Smoothie

Ingredients:

- 1 cup almond milk (or your preferred milk)
- 1/2 cup Greek yogurt (plain or vanilla)
- 2 tablespoons almond butter (or almond paste)
- 2 tablespoons cocoa powder (unsweetened)
- 1 tablespoon honey or maple syrup (adjust to taste)
- 1/4 cup shredded coconut (sweetened or unsweetened)
- 1/4 cup almonds (toasted or raw, plus extra for garnish)
- 1/2 teaspoon vanilla extract
- Ice cubes (as needed)

Instructions:

1. **Blend Ingredients:** In a blender, combine the almond milk, Greek yogurt, almond butter, cocoa powder, honey or maple syrup, shredded coconut, almonds, and vanilla extract.
2. **Add Ice:** Add a handful of ice cubes for a thicker, colder smoothie.
3. **Blend:** Blend on high until smooth and creamy. If the smoothie is too thick, add more almond milk to achieve your desired consistency.
4. **Taste and Adjust:** Taste the smoothie and adjust sweetness or cocoa flavor if needed by adding more honey or cocoa powder.
5. **Serve:** Pour the smoothie into a glass. Optionally, garnish with extra shredded coconut and almonds on top.

Enjoy your Almond Joy Smoothie! It's a rich and indulgent treat that combines the flavors of chocolate, almond, and coconut for a satisfying and creamy drink.

Peach Cobbler Shake

Ingredients:

- 1 cup fresh or frozen peach slices (peeled)
- 1/2 cup Greek yogurt (plain or vanilla)
- 1/2 cup milk (dairy or non-dairy, such as almond or oat milk)
- 1/4 cup rolled oats
- 1 tablespoon honey or maple syrup (adjust to taste)
- 1/2 teaspoon vanilla extract
- 1/2 teaspoon ground cinnamon
- 1/4 teaspoon ground nutmeg (optional, for extra spice)
- Ice cubes (as needed)
- Crumbled graham crackers or granola (optional, for garnish)

Instructions:

1. **Prepare Ingredients:** If using fresh peaches, peel and slice them. If using frozen peaches, they're ready to go.
2. **Blend Ingredients:** In a blender, combine the peach slices, Greek yogurt, milk, rolled oats, honey or maple syrup, vanilla extract, ground cinnamon, and ground nutmeg (if using).
3. **Add Ice:** Add a handful of ice cubes for a thicker, colder shake.
4. **Blend:** Blend on high until smooth and creamy. If the shake is too thick, add more milk to reach your desired consistency.
5. **Taste and Adjust:** Taste the shake and adjust sweetness or spice if needed by adding more honey or cinnamon.
6. **Serve:** Pour the shake into a glass. Optionally, garnish with crumbled graham crackers or granola for a touch of "cobbler" crunch.

Enjoy your Peach Cobbler Shake! It's a creamy and satisfying treat that combines the classic flavors of peach cobbler with the convenience of a shake.

Matcha Mango Meltdown

Ingredients:

- 1 cup fresh or frozen mango chunks
- 1 cup milk (dairy or non-dairy, such as almond or oat milk)
- 1/2 cup Greek yogurt (plain or vanilla)
- 1 teaspoon matcha powder
- 1 tablespoon honey or maple syrup (adjust to taste)
- 1/2 teaspoon vanilla extract
- Ice cubes (as needed)
- Mango slices or fresh mint (for garnish, optional)

Instructions:

1. **Prepare Ingredients:** If using fresh mango, peel and chop it. If using frozen mango, it's ready to go.
2. **Blend Ingredients:** In a blender, combine the mango chunks, milk, Greek yogurt, matcha powder, honey or maple syrup, and vanilla extract.
3. **Add Ice:** Add a handful of ice cubes for a thicker, colder shake.
4. **Blend:** Blend on high until smooth and creamy. If the shake is too thick, add more milk to achieve your desired consistency.
5. **Taste and Adjust:** Taste the shake and adjust sweetness if needed by adding more honey or maple syrup.
6. **Serve:** Pour the shake into a glass. Optionally, garnish with mango slices or fresh mint for a touch of extra flavor and visual appeal.

Enjoy your Matcha Mango Meltdown shake! It's a refreshing, creamy blend that combines the tropical sweetness of mango with the vibrant, earthy notes of matcha.

Coconut Vanilla Bean Dream

Ingredients:

- 1 cup coconut milk (full-fat or light, based on preference)
- 1/2 cup Greek yogurt (plain or vanilla)
- 1/4 cup shredded coconut (sweetened or unsweetened)
- 1 tablespoon honey or maple syrup (adjust to taste)
- 1 teaspoon vanilla bean paste or 1 teaspoon vanilla extract
- Ice cubes (as needed)
- Optional: 1/2 banana (for added creaminess)
- Optional: Extra shredded coconut (for garnish)

Instructions:

1. **Blend Ingredients:** In a blender, combine the coconut milk, Greek yogurt, shredded coconut, honey or maple syrup, and vanilla bean paste or vanilla extract. If using, add the banana for extra creaminess.
2. **Add Ice:** Add a handful of ice cubes for a thicker, colder shake.
3. **Blend:** Blend on high until smooth and creamy. If the shake is too thick, add more coconut milk to reach your desired consistency.
4. **Taste and Adjust:** Taste the shake and adjust sweetness if needed by adding more honey or maple syrup.
5. **Serve:** Pour the shake into a glass. Optionally, garnish with extra shredded coconut on top for added texture and visual appeal.

Enjoy your Coconut Vanilla Bean Dream shake! It's a creamy, tropical treat with a rich vanilla flavor that's perfect for a refreshing indulgence.

Salted Caramel Pretzel Shake

Ingredients:

- 1 cup milk (dairy or non-dairy, such as almond or oat milk)
- 1/2 cup Greek yogurt (plain or vanilla)
- 1/4 cup caramel sauce (store-bought or homemade)
- 1/4 cup crushed pretzels (plus extra for garnish)
- 1 tablespoon honey or maple syrup (adjust to taste)
- 1/4 teaspoon vanilla extract
- Ice cubes (as needed)
- Sea salt (for garnish, optional)

Instructions:

1. **Prepare Pretzels:** Crush the pretzels into small pieces. You can use a food processor or put them in a plastic bag and crush them with a rolling pin.
2. **Blend Ingredients:** In a blender, combine the milk, Greek yogurt, caramel sauce, crushed pretzels, honey or maple syrup, and vanilla extract.
3. **Add Ice:** Add a handful of ice cubes for a thicker, colder shake.
4. **Blend:** Blend on high until smooth and creamy. If the shake is too thick, add more milk to achieve your desired consistency.
5. **Taste and Adjust:** Taste the shake and adjust sweetness if needed by adding more honey or caramel sauce.
6. **Serve:** Pour the shake into a glass. Optionally, garnish with extra crushed pretzels and a sprinkle of sea salt on top for a sweet and salty touch.

Enjoy your Salted Caramel Pretzel Shake! It's a creamy, indulgent treat that beautifully blends the rich flavors of caramel with the crunchy, salty goodness of pretzels.

Avocado Banana Cream

Ingredients:

- 1 ripe avocado
- 1 ripe banana (peeled)
- 1/2 cup Greek yogurt (plain or vanilla)
- 1 cup milk (dairy or non-dairy, such as almond or oat milk)
- 1 tablespoon honey or maple syrup (adjust to taste)
- 1/2 teaspoon vanilla extract
- Ice cubes (as needed)
- Optional: 1 tablespoon chia seeds or flaxseeds (for added nutrition)

Instructions:

1. **Prepare Ingredients:** Scoop the flesh of the avocado into the blender. Peel and slice the banana.
2. **Blend Ingredients:** In a blender, combine the avocado, banana, Greek yogurt, milk, honey or maple syrup, and vanilla extract. If using, add chia seeds or flaxseeds.
3. **Add Ice:** Add a handful of ice cubes for a thicker, colder shake.
4. **Blend:** Blend on high until smooth and creamy. If the shake is too thick, add more milk to reach your desired consistency.
5. **Taste and Adjust:** Taste the shake and adjust sweetness if needed by adding more honey or maple syrup.
6. **Serve:** Pour the shake into a glass and enjoy immediately.

Enjoy your Avocado Banana Cream shake! It's a creamy, delicious treat with a smooth texture and a blend of subtle flavors that make it a nutritious and satisfying option.

Mocha Hazelnut Fantasy

Ingredients:

- 1 cup brewed coffee or espresso (cooled)
- 1/2 cup milk (dairy or non-dairy, such as almond or oat milk)
- 1/4 cup hazelnut butter (or hazelnut spread)
- 2 tablespoons cocoa powder (unsweetened)
- 1 tablespoon honey or maple syrup (adjust to taste)
- 1/2 teaspoon vanilla extract
- Ice cubes (as needed)
- Whipped cream (optional, for topping)
- Chopped hazelnuts or chocolate shavings (for garnish, optional)

Instructions:

1. **Prepare Coffee:** Brew a cup of coffee or espresso and let it cool to room temperature.
2. **Blend Ingredients:** In a blender, combine the cooled coffee, milk, hazelnut butter, cocoa powder, honey or maple syrup, and vanilla extract.
3. **Add Ice:** Add a handful of ice cubes for a thicker, colder shake.
4. **Blend:** Blend on high until smooth and creamy. If the shake is too thick, add more milk to reach your desired consistency.
5. **Taste and Adjust:** Taste the shake and adjust sweetness or cocoa flavor if needed by adding more honey or cocoa powder.
6. **Serve:** Pour the shake into a glass. Optionally, top with whipped cream and garnish with chopped hazelnuts or chocolate shavings.

Enjoy your Mocha Hazelnut Fantasy shake! It's a luxurious treat that combines the rich flavors of mocha and hazelnuts for a delightful and satisfying experience.

Berry Coconut Breeze

Ingredients:

- 1 cup mixed berries (fresh or frozen; blueberries, strawberries, raspberries, etc.)
- 1/2 cup coconut milk (full-fat or light, based on preference)
- 1/2 cup Greek yogurt (plain or vanilla)
- 1 tablespoon honey or maple syrup (adjust to taste)
- 1/4 cup shredded coconut (sweetened or unsweetened)
- 1/2 teaspoon vanilla extract
- Ice cubes (as needed)
- Fresh berries or a sprinkle of shredded coconut (for garnish, optional)

Instructions:

1. **Prepare Berries:** If using fresh berries, wash them thoroughly. If using frozen berries, they're ready to go.
2. **Blend Ingredients:** In a blender, combine the mixed berries, coconut milk, Greek yogurt, honey or maple syrup, shredded coconut, and vanilla extract.
3. **Add Ice:** Add a handful of ice cubes for a thicker, colder shake.
4. **Blend:** Blend on high until smooth and creamy. If the shake is too thick, add more coconut milk to reach your desired consistency.
5. **Taste and Adjust:** Taste the shake and adjust sweetness if needed by adding more honey or maple syrup.
6. **Serve:** Pour the shake into a glass. Optionally, garnish with fresh berries or a sprinkle of shredded coconut.

Enjoy your Berry Coconut Breeze shake! It's a deliciously creamy and tropical blend that combines the sweet flavors of mixed berries with the rich, nutty taste of coconut.

Chocolate Peanut Butter Crunch

Ingredients:

- 1 cup milk (dairy or non-dairy, such as almond or oat milk)
- 1/2 cup Greek yogurt (plain or vanilla)
- 2 tablespoons peanut butter (creamy or chunky, based on preference)
- 2 tablespoons cocoa powder (unsweetened)
- 1 tablespoon honey or maple syrup (adjust to taste)
- 1/4 teaspoon vanilla extract
- 1/4 cup granola or crushed peanuts (for added crunch)
- Ice cubes (as needed)
- Optional: 1/4 cup chocolate chips (for extra chocolatey goodness)

Instructions:

1. **Blend Ingredients:** In a blender, combine the milk, Greek yogurt, peanut butter, cocoa powder, honey or maple syrup, and vanilla extract. If using, add the chocolate chips.
2. **Add Ice:** Add a handful of ice cubes for a thicker, colder shake.
3. **Blend:** Blend on high until smooth and creamy. If the shake is too thick, add more milk to reach your desired consistency.
4. **Add Crunch:** Once blended, stir in the granola or crushed peanuts for a crunchy texture. You can also blend them in if you prefer a more uniform texture.
5. **Taste and Adjust:** Taste the shake and adjust sweetness or chocolate flavor if needed by adding more honey or cocoa powder.
6. **Serve:** Pour the shake into a glass. Optionally, top with extra granola or peanuts for added crunch.

Enjoy your Chocolate Peanut Butter Crunch shake! It's a rich and creamy treat with a satisfying crunch, perfect for a chocolatey and nutty indulgence.

Apple Cinnamon Delight

Ingredients:

- 1 cup apple slices (peeled, cored, and chopped; fresh or frozen)
- 1/2 cup Greek yogurt (plain or vanilla)
- 1/2 cup milk (dairy or non-dairy, such as almond or oat milk)
- 1 tablespoon honey or maple syrup (adjust to taste)
- 1/2 teaspoon ground cinnamon
- 1/4 teaspoon vanilla extract
- Ice cubes (as needed)
- Optional: 1/4 cup rolled oats (for added texture and nutrition)
- Optional: Fresh apple slices or a sprinkle of cinnamon (for garnish)

Instructions:

1. **Prepare Apples:** If using fresh apples, peel, core, and chop them. If using frozen apples, they're ready to go.
2. **Blend Ingredients:** In a blender, combine the apple slices, Greek yogurt, milk, honey or maple syrup, ground cinnamon, and vanilla extract. If using, add the rolled oats for extra texture and nutrition.
3. **Add Ice:** Add a handful of ice cubes for a thicker, colder shake.
4. **Blend:** Blend on high until smooth and creamy. If the shake is too thick, add more milk to achieve your desired consistency.
5. **Taste and Adjust:** Taste the shake and adjust sweetness or spice if needed by adding more honey or cinnamon.
6. **Serve:** Pour the shake into a glass. Optionally, garnish with fresh apple slices or a sprinkle of cinnamon.

Enjoy your Apple Cinnamon Delight shake! It's a creamy and flavorful treat that brings together the classic flavors of apple and cinnamon for a comforting and satisfying drink.

Cherry Almond Bliss

Ingredients:

- 1 cup fresh or frozen cherries (pitted)
- 1/2 cup Greek yogurt (plain or vanilla)
- 1/2 cup almond milk (or your preferred milk)
- 2 tablespoons almond butter (or almond paste)
- 1 tablespoon honey or maple syrup (adjust to taste)
- 1/4 teaspoon almond extract
- 1/4 cup sliced almonds (for added crunch)
- Ice cubes (as needed)
- Optional: Extra cherries or almond slices (for garnish)

Instructions:

1. **Prepare Cherries:** If using fresh cherries, pit and chop them. If using frozen cherries, they're ready to go.
2. **Blend Ingredients:** In a blender, combine the cherries, Greek yogurt, almond milk, almond butter, honey or maple syrup, and almond extract.
3. **Add Ice:** Add a handful of ice cubes for a thicker, colder shake.
4. **Blend:** Blend on high until smooth and creamy. If the shake is too thick, add more almond milk to achieve your desired consistency.
5. **Add Crunch:** Once blended, stir in the sliced almonds for a crunchy texture. You can also blend them in if you prefer a more uniform texture.
6. **Taste and Adjust:** Taste the shake and adjust sweetness or almond flavor if needed by adding more honey or almond extract.
7. **Serve:** Pour the shake into a glass. Optionally, garnish with extra cherries or almond slices.

Enjoy your Cherry Almond Bliss shake! It's a creamy, nutty treat with a perfect blend of sweet cherries and rich almond flavor.

Lemon Basil Mint Smoothie

Ingredients:

- 1 cup fresh spinach or kale (optional, for added nutrition)
- 1/2 cup fresh basil leaves
- 1/4 cup fresh mint leaves
- 1 cup lemon yogurt (plain or vanilla)
- 1/2 cup lemonade (store-bought or homemade)
- 1/2 cup water (or more, to adjust consistency)
- 1 tablespoon honey or agave syrup (adjust to taste)
- 1/2 lemon, juiced (about 2 tablespoons of lemon juice)
- Ice cubes (as needed)
- Optional: Lemon slices or extra mint leaves (for garnish)

Instructions:

1. **Prepare Ingredients:** Wash the spinach or kale (if using), basil leaves, and mint leaves. Juice the lemon.
2. **Blend Ingredients:** In a blender, combine the spinach or kale (if using), basil leaves, mint leaves, lemon yogurt, lemonade, water, honey or agave syrup, and lemon juice.
3. **Add Ice:** Add a handful of ice cubes for a thicker, colder smoothie.
4. **Blend:** Blend on high until smooth and creamy. If the smoothie is too thick, add more water or lemonade to achieve your desired consistency.
5. **Taste and Adjust:** Taste the smoothie and adjust sweetness or tartness if needed by adding more honey or lemon juice.
6. **Serve:** Pour the smoothie into a glass. Optionally, garnish with lemon slices or extra mint leaves for a touch of visual appeal.

Enjoy your Lemon Basil Mint Smoothie! It's a light, refreshing blend with a hint of herbal notes from basil and mint, making it perfect for a cooling and invigorating drink.

Maple Pecan Protein Shake

Ingredients:

- 1 cup milk (dairy or non-dairy, such as almond or oat milk)
- 1/2 cup Greek yogurt (plain or vanilla)
- 2 tablespoons pecan butter (or pecan paste)
- 1 tablespoon pure maple syrup
- 1 scoop vanilla protein powder (your choice of brand)
- 1/4 teaspoon vanilla extract
- 1/4 cup chopped pecans (for added crunch)
- Ice cubes (as needed)

Instructions:

1. **Blend Ingredients:** In a blender, combine the milk, Greek yogurt, pecan butter, maple syrup, vanilla protein powder, and vanilla extract.
2. **Add Ice:** Add a handful of ice cubes for a thicker, colder shake.
3. **Blend:** Blend on high until smooth and creamy. If the shake is too thick, add more milk to achieve your desired consistency.
4. **Add Crunch:** Once blended, stir in the chopped pecans for a crunchy texture. You can also blend them in if you prefer a more uniform texture.
5. **Taste and Adjust:** Taste the shake and adjust sweetness if needed by adding more maple syrup.
6. **Serve:** Pour the shake into a glass and enjoy immediately.

Enjoy your Maple Pecan Protein Shake! It's a creamy and nutty shake with a delightful maple flavor, perfect for a nutritious and satisfying treat.

Sweet Potato Pie Shake

Ingredients:

- 1 cup cooked and cooled sweet potato (peeled and mashed)
- 1/2 cup Greek yogurt (plain or vanilla)
- 1/2 cup milk (dairy or non-dairy, such as almond or oat milk)
- 1 tablespoon maple syrup or honey (adjust to taste)
- 1/2 teaspoon ground cinnamon
- 1/4 teaspoon ground nutmeg
- 1/4 teaspoon vanilla extract
- Ice cubes (as needed)
- Optional: 1/4 cup rolled oats (for added texture and nutrition)
- Optional: Whipped cream and a sprinkle of cinnamon (for garnish)

Instructions:

1. **Prepare Sweet Potato:** If not using pre-cooked sweet potato, bake or boil the sweet potato until tender. Let it cool, then peel and mash.
2. **Blend Ingredients:** In a blender, combine the mashed sweet potato, Greek yogurt, milk, maple syrup or honey, ground cinnamon, ground nutmeg, and vanilla extract. If using, add the rolled oats for extra texture and nutrition.
3. **Add Ice:** Add a handful of ice cubes for a thicker, colder shake.
4. **Blend:** Blend on high until smooth and creamy. If the shake is too thick, add more milk to achieve your desired consistency.
5. **Taste and Adjust:** Taste the shake and adjust sweetness or spice if needed by adding more maple syrup or cinnamon.
6. **Serve:** Pour the shake into a glass. Optionally, top with whipped cream and a sprinkle of cinnamon for a touch of indulgence.

Enjoy your Sweet Potato Pie Shake! It's a rich, creamy shake with all the comforting flavors of sweet potato pie, perfect for a fall-inspired treat or a comforting snack.

Pomegranate Acai Burst

Ingredients:

- 1 cup pomegranate juice (100% juice, no added sugar)
- 1/2 cup frozen acai berries (or acai puree)
- 1/2 cup Greek yogurt (plain or vanilla)
- 1/2 banana (peeled)
- 1 tablespoon honey or agave syrup (adjust to taste)
- 1/4 cup fresh pomegranate seeds (optional, for garnish)
- Ice cubes (as needed)
- Optional: 1 tablespoon chia seeds or flaxseeds (for added nutrition)

Instructions:

1. **Blend Ingredients:** In a blender, combine the pomegranate juice, frozen acai berries, Greek yogurt, banana, and honey or agave syrup. If using, add chia seeds or flaxseeds.
2. **Add Ice:** Add a handful of ice cubes for a thicker, colder shake.
3. **Blend:** Blend on high until smooth and creamy. If the shake is too thick, add more pomegranate juice to achieve your desired consistency.
4. **Taste and Adjust:** Taste the shake and adjust sweetness if needed by adding more honey or agave syrup.
5. **Serve:** Pour the shake into a glass. Optionally, garnish with fresh pomegranate seeds for a burst of color and texture.

Enjoy your Pomegranate Acai Burst shake! It's a refreshing, antioxidant-rich treat that combines the tangy flavor of pomegranate with the superfood benefits of acai berries.

Strawberry Rhubarb Shake

Ingredients:

- 1 cup fresh or frozen strawberries (hulled)
- 1/2 cup chopped rhubarb (fresh or frozen)
- 1/2 cup Greek yogurt (plain or vanilla)
- 1/2 cup milk (dairy or non-dairy, such as almond or oat milk)
- 1-2 tablespoons honey or maple syrup (adjust to taste)
- 1/4 teaspoon vanilla extract
- Ice cubes (as needed)
- Optional: 1 tablespoon chia seeds or flaxseeds (for added nutrition)

Instructions:

1. **Prepare Rhubarb:** If using fresh rhubarb, chop it into small pieces. If using frozen rhubarb, it's ready to go. To soften the rhubarb, you can cook it lightly with a little water and sweetener until tender, then cool it before using. Alternatively, you can use rhubarb compote or preserves.
2. **Blend Ingredients:** In a blender, combine the strawberries, chopped rhubarb, Greek yogurt, milk, honey or maple syrup, and vanilla extract. If using, add chia seeds or flaxseeds.
3. **Add Ice:** Add a handful of ice cubes for a thicker, colder shake.
4. **Blend:** Blend on high until smooth and creamy. If the shake is too thick, add more milk to achieve your desired consistency.
5. **Taste and Adjust:** Taste the shake and adjust sweetness or tartness if needed by adding more honey or syrup.
6. **Serve:** Pour the shake into a glass and enjoy immediately.

Enjoy your Strawberry Rhubarb Shake! It's a refreshing and creamy treat that combines the sweet flavor of strawberries with the tangy kick of rhubarb, perfect for a delightful and unique shake experience.

Mint Chocolate Chip Shake

Ingredients:

- 1 cup milk (dairy or non-dairy, such as almond or oat milk)
- 1/2 cup Greek yogurt (plain or vanilla)
- 1/4 cup fresh mint leaves (or 1 teaspoon mint extract)
- 1/4 cup mini chocolate chips (or chopped dark chocolate)
- 2 tablespoons honey or maple syrup (adjust to taste)
- 1/4 teaspoon vanilla extract
- Ice cubes (as needed)

Instructions:

1. **Prepare Mint:** If using fresh mint leaves, wash them thoroughly. If using mint extract, you can skip this step.
2. **Blend Ingredients:** In a blender, combine the milk, Greek yogurt, fresh mint leaves (if using), chocolate chips, honey or maple syrup, and vanilla extract.
3. **Add Ice:** Add a handful of ice cubes for a thicker, colder shake.
4. **Blend:** Blend on high until smooth and creamy. If the shake is too thick, add more milk to achieve your desired consistency.
5. **Add Chocolate Chips:** Once blended, stir in additional chocolate chips if you like extra chocolatey chunks, or blend briefly to incorporate them if you prefer a more uniform texture.
6. **Taste and Adjust:** Taste the shake and adjust sweetness or mint flavor if needed by adding more honey or mint extract.
7. **Serve:** Pour the shake into a glass and enjoy immediately. Optionally, garnish with extra chocolate chips or a sprig of mint for added flair.

Enjoy your Mint Chocolate Chip Shake! It's a creamy and indulgent treat with a delightful blend of refreshing mint and rich chocolate flavors.

Spiced Orange Creamsicle

Ingredients:

- 1 cup orange juice (preferably fresh or 100% juice)
- 1/2 cup Greek yogurt (plain or vanilla)
- 1/2 cup vanilla ice cream (or frozen yogurt for a lighter option)
- 1/4 teaspoon ground cinnamon
- 1/4 teaspoon ground nutmeg
- 1/4 teaspoon vanilla extract
- Ice cubes (as needed)
- Optional: 1 tablespoon honey or maple syrup (adjust to taste)
- Optional: Orange zest or cinnamon stick (for garnish)

Instructions:

1. **Blend Ingredients:** In a blender, combine the orange juice, Greek yogurt, vanilla ice cream, ground cinnamon, ground nutmeg, and vanilla extract. If using, add honey or maple syrup for extra sweetness.
2. **Add Ice:** Add a handful of ice cubes for a thicker, colder shake.
3. **Blend:** Blend on high until smooth and creamy. If the shake is too thick, add a little more orange juice to reach your desired consistency.
4. **Taste and Adjust:** Taste the shake and adjust sweetness or spice if needed by adding more honey or spices.
5. **Serve:** Pour the shake into a glass. Optionally, garnish with a sprinkle of orange zest or a cinnamon stick for a touch of elegance.

Enjoy your Spiced Orange Creamsicle shake! It's a creamy, nostalgic treat with a delightful blend of citrusy orange and warm spices, perfect for a refreshing and satisfying drink.

Tropical Guava Dream

Ingredients:

- 1 cup guava juice (or fresh guava, peeled and chopped)
- 1/2 cup pineapple chunks (fresh or frozen)
- 1/2 cup coconut milk (full-fat or light, based on preference)
- 1/2 cup Greek yogurt (plain or vanilla)
- 1 tablespoon honey or agave syrup (adjust to taste)
- 1/4 teaspoon vanilla extract
- Ice cubes (as needed)
- Optional: 1 tablespoon chia seeds or flaxseeds (for added nutrition)

Instructions:

1. **Prepare Guava:** If using fresh guava, peel and chop it into pieces. If using guava juice, you can skip this step.
2. **Blend Ingredients:** In a blender, combine the guava juice (or fresh guava), pineapple chunks, coconut milk, Greek yogurt, honey or agave syrup, and vanilla extract. If using, add chia seeds or flaxseeds.
3. **Add Ice:** Add a handful of ice cubes for a thicker, colder shake.
4. **Blend:** Blend on high until smooth and creamy. If the shake is too thick, add more guava juice or coconut milk to achieve your desired consistency.
5. **Taste and Adjust:** Taste the shake and adjust sweetness if needed by adding more honey or agave syrup.
6. **Serve:** Pour the shake into a glass and enjoy immediately.

Enjoy your Tropical Guava Dream shake! It's a creamy and exotic treat that combines the sweet flavors of guava, pineapple, and coconut for a tropical escape in a glass.

Vanilla Nutmeg Bliss

Ingredients:

- 1 cup milk (dairy or non-dairy, such as almond or oat milk)
- 1/2 cup Greek yogurt (plain or vanilla)
- 1 tablespoon vanilla extract
- 1/4 teaspoon ground nutmeg (or more to taste)
- 1-2 tablespoons honey or maple syrup (adjust to taste)
- Ice cubes (as needed)
- Optional: 1/4 cup rolled oats (for added texture and nutrition)

Instructions:

1. **Blend Ingredients:** In a blender, combine the milk, Greek yogurt, vanilla extract, ground nutmeg, and honey or maple syrup. If using, add rolled oats for extra texture and nutrition.
2. **Add Ice:** Add a handful of ice cubes for a thicker, colder shake.
3. **Blend:** Blend on high until smooth and creamy. If the shake is too thick, add more milk to reach your desired consistency.
4. **Taste and Adjust:** Taste the shake and adjust sweetness or nutmeg flavor if needed by adding more honey or nutmeg.
5. **Serve:** Pour the shake into a glass. Optionally, garnish with a sprinkle of nutmeg on top for added aroma.

Enjoy your Vanilla Nutmeg Bliss shake! It's a creamy, soothing treat with a lovely blend of vanilla and nutmeg, perfect for a comforting and indulgent drink.

Raspberry Coconut Fusion

Ingredients:

- 1 cup fresh or frozen raspberries
- 1/2 cup coconut milk (full-fat or light, based on preference)
- 1/2 cup Greek yogurt (plain or vanilla)
- 1 tablespoon honey or agave syrup (adjust to taste)
- 1/4 cup shredded coconut (sweetened or unsweetened)
- 1/4 teaspoon vanilla extract
- Ice cubes (as needed)
- Optional: Fresh raspberries or extra shredded coconut (for garnish)

Instructions:

1. **Blend Ingredients:** In a blender, combine the raspberries, coconut milk, Greek yogurt, honey or agave syrup, shredded coconut, and vanilla extract.
2. **Add Ice:** Add a handful of ice cubes for a thicker, colder shake.
3. **Blend:** Blend on high until smooth and creamy. If the shake is too thick, add more coconut milk to reach your desired consistency.
4. **Taste and Adjust:** Taste the shake and adjust sweetness if needed by adding more honey or agave syrup.
5. **Serve:** Pour the shake into a glass. Optionally, garnish with fresh raspberries or a sprinkle of shredded coconut.

Enjoy your Raspberry Coconut Fusion shake! It's a deliciously creamy and fruity treat that combines the tartness of raspberries with the tropical flavor of coconut for a refreshing and indulgent experience.

White Chocolate Raspberry

Ingredients:

- 1 cup fresh or frozen raspberries
- 1/2 cup white chocolate chips or chopped white chocolate
- 1/2 cup milk (dairy or non-dairy, such as almond or oat milk)
- 1/2 cup Greek yogurt (plain or vanilla)
- 1 tablespoon honey or maple syrup (adjust to taste)
- 1/4 teaspoon vanilla extract
- Ice cubes (as needed)
- Optional: Whipped cream and extra white chocolate shavings (for garnish)

Instructions:

1. **Melt White Chocolate:** Melt the white chocolate chips or chopped white chocolate. You can do this in the microwave in 20-second intervals, stirring between each, or using a double boiler on the stove. Allow it to cool slightly before using.
2. **Blend Ingredients:** In a blender, combine the raspberries, melted white chocolate, milk, Greek yogurt, honey or maple syrup, and vanilla extract.
3. **Add Ice:** Add a handful of ice cubes for a thicker, colder shake.
4. **Blend:** Blend on high until smooth and creamy. If the shake is too thick, add more milk to reach your desired consistency.
5. **Taste and Adjust:** Taste the shake and adjust sweetness if needed by adding more honey or maple syrup.
6. **Serve:** Pour the shake into a glass. Optionally, top with whipped cream and garnish with extra white chocolate shavings.

Enjoy your White Chocolate Raspberry Shake! It's a luscious, creamy treat with a delightful blend of sweet white chocolate and tart raspberries, perfect for a decadent indulgence.

Blackberry Lemon Basil

Ingredients:

- 1 cup fresh or frozen blackberries
- 1/2 cup Greek yogurt (plain or vanilla)
- 1/2 cup milk (dairy or non-dairy, such as almond or oat milk)
- 1 tablespoon honey or agave syrup (adjust to taste)
- 1 tablespoon fresh lemon juice (about 1/2 lemon)
- 1/4 cup fresh basil leaves
- Ice cubes (as needed)
- Optional: Lemon zest or extra basil leaves (for garnish)

Instructions:

1. **Prepare Ingredients:** If using fresh blackberries, wash them thoroughly. If using frozen blackberries, they're ready to go. Wash the basil leaves and juice the lemon.
2. **Blend Ingredients:** In a blender, combine the blackberries, Greek yogurt, milk, honey or agave syrup, lemon juice, and basil leaves.
3. **Add Ice:** Add a handful of ice cubes for a thicker, colder shake.
4. **Blend:** Blend on high until smooth and creamy. If the shake is too thick, add more milk to achieve your desired consistency.
5. **Taste and Adjust:** Taste the shake and adjust sweetness or lemon flavor if needed by adding more honey or lemon juice.
6. **Serve:** Pour the shake into a glass. Optionally, garnish with lemon zest or extra basil leaves for a touch of elegance.

Enjoy your Blackberry Lemon Basil Shake! It's a vibrant and refreshing treat that combines the fruity sweetness of blackberries with the bright, zesty notes of lemon and the fragrant touch of basil.

Chocolate Banana Nut

Ingredients:

- 1 banana (peeled and sliced)
- 1 cup milk (dairy or non-dairy, such as almond or oat milk)
- 2 tablespoons cocoa powder (unsweetened)
- 2 tablespoons nut butter (such as almond butter or peanut butter)
- 1 tablespoon honey or maple syrup (adjust to taste)
- 1/4 teaspoon vanilla extract
- 1/4 cup chopped nuts (such as almonds or walnuts)
- Ice cubes (as needed)
- Optional: 1 scoop chocolate protein powder (for an extra protein boost)

Instructions:

1. **Blend Ingredients:** In a blender, combine the banana, milk, cocoa powder, nut butter, honey or maple syrup, and vanilla extract. If using, add the chocolate protein powder.
2. **Add Ice:** Add a handful of ice cubes for a thicker, colder shake.
3. **Blend:** Blend on high until smooth and creamy. If the shake is too thick, add more milk to achieve your desired consistency.
4. **Add Nuts:** Once blended, stir in the chopped nuts for a crunchy texture. You can also blend them in if you prefer a more uniform texture.
5. **Taste and Adjust:** Taste the shake and adjust sweetness or chocolate flavor if needed by adding more honey or cocoa powder.
6. **Serve:** Pour the shake into a glass and enjoy immediately.

Enjoy your Chocolate Banana Nut Shake! It's a creamy, indulgent treat with the perfect combination of chocolate and banana flavors, enhanced by the satisfying crunch of nuts.

Fig and Walnut Shake

Ingredients:

- 1 cup fresh or dried figs (stems removed and chopped if dried)
- 1/2 cup Greek yogurt (plain or vanilla)
- 1/2 cup milk (dairy or non-dairy, such as almond or oat milk)
- 1/4 cup walnuts (chopped)
- 1 tablespoon honey or maple syrup (adjust to taste)
- 1/4 teaspoon vanilla extract
- Ice cubes (as needed)
- Optional: Extra chopped walnuts or fig slices (for garnish)

Instructions:

1. **Prepare Figs:** If using dried figs, soak them in warm water for about 10 minutes to soften, then drain. If using fresh figs, just chop them into smaller pieces.
2. **Blend Ingredients:** In a blender, combine the figs, Greek yogurt, milk, chopped walnuts, honey or maple syrup, and vanilla extract.
3. **Add Ice:** Add a handful of ice cubes for a thicker, colder shake.
4. **Blend:** Blend on high until smooth and creamy. If the shake is too thick, add more milk to achieve your desired consistency.
5. **Add Walnuts:** Once blended, stir in additional chopped walnuts for added texture, or blend them in if you prefer a more uniform texture.
6. **Taste and Adjust:** Taste the shake and adjust sweetness if needed by adding more honey or maple syrup.
7. **Serve:** Pour the shake into a glass. Optionally, garnish with extra chopped walnuts or fig slices.

Enjoy your Fig and Walnut Shake! It's a creamy, nutritious treat with a delightful blend of sweet figs and nutty walnuts, perfect for a satisfying snack or breakfast.

Gingerbread Protein Shake

Ingredients:

- 1 cup milk (dairy or non-dairy, such as almond or oat milk)
- 1/2 cup Greek yogurt (plain or vanilla)
- 1 scoop vanilla or gingerbread protein powder (optional, but adds extra protein)
- 1 tablespoon molasses or honey (adjust to taste)
- 1/2 teaspoon ground ginger
- 1/2 teaspoon ground cinnamon
- 1/4 teaspoon ground nutmeg
- 1/4 teaspoon vanilla extract
- Ice cubes (as needed)
- Optional: 1/4 cup rolled oats (for added texture and nutrition)

Instructions:

1. **Blend Ingredients:** In a blender, combine the milk, Greek yogurt, protein powder (if using), molasses or honey, ground ginger, ground cinnamon, ground nutmeg, and vanilla extract. If using, add rolled oats for extra texture.
2. **Add Ice:** Add a handful of ice cubes for a thicker, colder shake.
3. **Blend:** Blend on high until smooth and creamy. If the shake is too thick, add more milk to achieve your desired consistency.
4. **Taste and Adjust:** Taste the shake and adjust sweetness or spice levels if needed by adding more molasses, honey, or spices.
5. **Serve:** Pour the shake into a glass and enjoy immediately.

Enjoy your Gingerbread Protein Shake! It's a warm, spiced treat with the nostalgic flavors of gingerbread, perfect for a post-workout snack or a cozy treat.

Coconut Matcha Bliss

Ingredients:

- 1 cup coconut milk (full-fat or light, based on preference)
- 1/2 cup Greek yogurt (plain or vanilla)
- 1 teaspoon matcha green tea powder
- 1 tablespoon honey or maple syrup (adjust to taste)
- 1/4 teaspoon vanilla extract
- Ice cubes (as needed)
- Optional: 1 tablespoon shredded coconut (for added texture)
- Optional: 1/2 banana (for extra creaminess and natural sweetness)

Instructions:

1. **Blend Ingredients:** In a blender, combine the coconut milk, Greek yogurt, matcha powder, honey or maple syrup, and vanilla extract. If using, add shredded coconut and/or banana.
2. **Add Ice:** Add a handful of ice cubes for a thicker, colder shake.
3. **Blend:** Blend on high until smooth and creamy. If the shake is too thick, add more coconut milk to achieve your desired consistency.
4. **Taste and Adjust:** Taste the shake and adjust sweetness or matcha flavor if needed by adding more honey or matcha powder.
5. **Serve:** Pour the shake into a glass and enjoy immediately.

Enjoy your Coconut Matcha Bliss Shake! It's a creamy, tropical treat with the vibrant, earthy flavor of matcha and the smooth richness of coconut, perfect for a refreshing and energizing drink.

Spicy Mango Tango

Ingredients:

- 1 cup fresh or frozen mango chunks
- 1/2 cup Greek yogurt (plain or vanilla)
- 1/2 cup milk (dairy or non-dairy, such as almond or oat milk)
- 1 tablespoon honey or agave syrup (adjust to taste)
- 1/4 teaspoon cayenne pepper (or more to taste)
- 1/4 teaspoon ground ginger
- 1/4 teaspoon ground cinnamon
- 1/4 teaspoon vanilla extract
- Ice cubes (as needed)
- Optional: 1/2 lime (juiced for a tangy twist)

Instructions:

1. **Blend Ingredients:** In a blender, combine the mango chunks, Greek yogurt, milk, honey or agave syrup, cayenne pepper, ground ginger, ground cinnamon, and vanilla extract. If using, add lime juice for extra tanginess.
2. **Add Ice:** Add a handful of ice cubes for a thicker, colder shake.
3. **Blend:** Blend on high until smooth and creamy. If the shake is too thick, add more milk to reach your desired consistency.
4. **Taste and Adjust:** Taste the shake and adjust sweetness or spice if needed by adding more honey or cayenne pepper.
5. **Serve:** Pour the shake into a glass and enjoy immediately.

Enjoy your Spicy Mango Tango Shake! It's a unique blend of sweet mango and spicy heat, offering a refreshing and invigorating treat with a delightful kick.

Blueberry Yogurt Smoothie

Ingredients:

- 1 cup fresh or frozen blueberries
- 1/2 cup Greek yogurt (plain or vanilla)
- 1/2 cup milk (dairy or non-dairy, such as almond or oat milk)
- 1 tablespoon honey or maple syrup (adjust to taste)
- 1/4 teaspoon vanilla extract
- Ice cubes (as needed)
- Optional: 1 tablespoon chia seeds or flaxseeds (for added nutrition)

Instructions:

1. **Blend Ingredients:** In a blender, combine the blueberries, Greek yogurt, milk, honey or maple syrup, and vanilla extract. If using, add chia seeds or flaxseeds.
2. **Add Ice:** Add a handful of ice cubes for a thicker, colder smoothie.
3. **Blend:** Blend on high until smooth and creamy. If the smoothie is too thick, add more milk to achieve your desired consistency.
4. **Taste and Adjust:** Taste the smoothie and adjust sweetness if needed by adding more honey or maple syrup.
5. **Serve:** Pour the smoothie into a glass and enjoy immediately.

Enjoy your Blueberry Yogurt Smoothie! It's a creamy and nutritious drink that highlights the sweet-tart flavor of blueberries, perfect for a quick breakfast or a refreshing snack.

Nutty Almond Joy Shake

Ingredients:

- 1 cup milk (dairy or non-dairy, such as almond or coconut milk)
- 1/2 cup Greek yogurt (plain or vanilla)
- 2 tablespoons cocoa powder (unsweetened)
- 2 tablespoons almond butter (or peanut butter)
- 1/4 cup shredded coconut (sweetened or unsweetened)
- 1 tablespoon honey or maple syrup (adjust to taste)
- 1/4 teaspoon vanilla extract
- 1/4 cup chopped almonds (for added texture)
- Ice cubes (as needed)
- Optional: 1 scoop chocolate protein powder (for extra protein)

Instructions:

1. **Blend Ingredients:** In a blender, combine the milk, Greek yogurt, cocoa powder, almond butter, shredded coconut, honey or maple syrup, and vanilla extract. If using, add chocolate protein powder.
2. **Add Ice:** Add a handful of ice cubes for a thicker, colder shake.
3. **Blend:** Blend on high until smooth and creamy. If the shake is too thick, add more milk to achieve your desired consistency.
4. **Add Almonds:** Once blended, stir in the chopped almonds for added crunch, or blend briefly to incorporate them.
5. **Taste and Adjust:** Taste the shake and adjust sweetness or flavor if needed by adding more honey or cocoa powder.
6. **Serve:** Pour the shake into a glass and enjoy immediately.

Enjoy your Nutty Almond Joy Shake! It's a creamy and indulgent treat with a delightful combination of chocolate, almond, and coconut flavors, perfect for a satisfying and flavorful snack or dessert.

www.ingramcontent.com/pod-product-compliance
Lightning Source LLC
LaVergne TN
LVHW081327060526
838201LV00055B/2508